I0162176

UNDERCOVER NUNS

MERLE PYKE

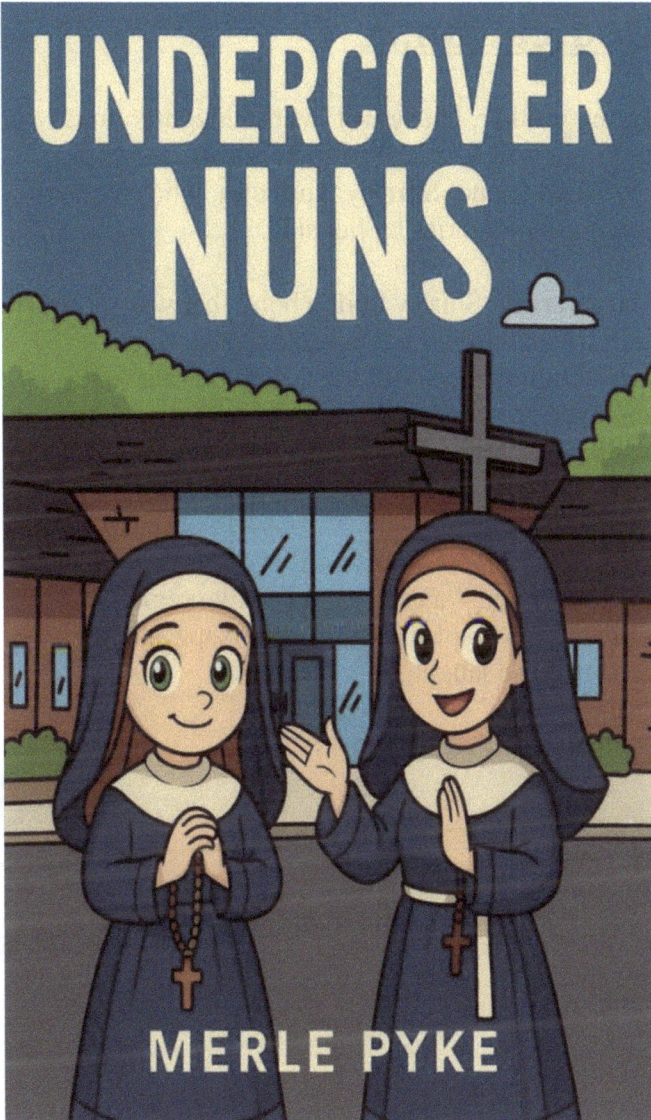

Written by Merle Pyke

Illustrations by Stacey Johnson

Undercover Nuns

Dedication:

To my mother, **Margaret**, whose laughter, love, and light will forever live in my heart, and to her cherished friend, **Shirley Andrews**, who shared in countless memories by her side.

Margaret and Shirley built a bond that was more than friendship—it was a lifelong sisterhood, a connection woven with trust, humour, and unwavering support. Through every joy and challenge, they stood together, creating moments that will never be forgotten.

This book, *Undercover Nuns*, is a tribute to that beautiful bond—a celebration of two remarkable women whose spirits continue to inspire love, strength, and laughter.

With all my love and gratitude,

Merle

Introduction:

Undercover Nuns

In the quiet city of Cornwall, no one expected that two nuns—Sister Margaret and Sister Shirley—would become the most unlikely heroes in the fight against organized crime. Known at St. Peter's Parish for their mischievous streak and less-than-holy fundraising tactics, these two sisters are far from your typical women of the cloth. When their questionable behavior finally gets them kicked out of the parish, Mother Superior orders them to "go out into the community and spread the good word."

But spreading the good word isn't exactly in their nature. Instead, Margaret and Shirley find themselves stumbling into one outrageous scheme after another. From selling "miracle water" that's just tap water, to accidentally ripping off the mob during a diamond deal, their antics quickly spiral out of control. With the mob out for revenge and the RCMP Mob Division hot on their heels, the sisters must rely on quick wit, bold lies, and a surprising knack for chaos to survive.

What follows is a rollercoaster of con jobs, car chases, and holy hijinks as the sisters form an uneasy alliance with Detective Louie

Laframboise to take down a dangerous crime syndicate. Along the way, they discover that being "undercover" might just be their true calling—especially when diamonds, double-crosses, and redemption are on the line.

Undercover Nuns is a fast-paced, laugh-out-loud adventure that blends crime, comedy, and just a touch of divine mischief. Whether they're saving souls or stealing diamonds, one thing is certain: Sister Margaret and Sister Shirley will stop at nothing to get the job done... even if it means bending the Ten Commandments along the way.

Table of Contents

Chapter 1

Holy Hustlers

The bells of St. Peter's Parish rang with their usual solemnity, echoing across the quiet city of Cornwall. Inside the grand church, sunlight filtered through stained glass, painting the stone floor with brilliant shades of crimson and gold. Sister Margaret sat in the front pew, twirling a rosary between her fingers like a poker chip, while Sister Shirley counted the collection money behind the altar.

Undercover Nuns

"Two hundred, forty... fifty... seventy," Shirley mumbled, licking her thumb and flipping bills. "Not bad for a Wednesday. People must be feeling guilty this week."

Margaret smirked, leaning back with her habit slipping slightly off her head. "Guilt is the church's best business partner, my dear. It's practically a renewable resource."

Shirley giggled, her cheeks flushing pink. "Maybe next week we should guilt them about the roof repairs again. Worked last month."

"The roof is fine," Margaret said, shrugging. "But as long as Father Maloney keeps preaching about the fire and brimstone, these people will pay to avoid eternal barbecuing. We're practically doing them a service."

Before Shirley could respond, the heavy wooden doors creaked open. The sound reverberated through the nave, a low, ominous groan that could make any sinner sit up straight. Mother Superior Marie entered with the measured grace of a judge walking into a courtroom. Her piercing brown eyes could silence a room, and her rosary beads clicked with every step like a chain of divine judgment.

"Margaret. Shirley," she said, her voice firm as oak. "We need to talk."

Shirley froze mid-count. Margaret, ever the bold one, offered a half-smile. "Mother Superior, what a lovely surprise. Have you come to bless our charity efforts?"

"Bless?" Mother Superior's gaze dropped to the overflowing collection box. "Or investigate?" Her tone was colder than the marble altar.

Mother Superior Marie led them into her office, a small, austere room with only a desk, a crucifix on the wall, and two chairs that looked as uncomfortable as confession booths. She motioned for them to sit.

"I've been looking through the parish financial records," Marie began, folding her hands. "Something doesn't add up. We raised twelve hundred dollars for the orphanage this month. Yet the orphanage reports only receiving four hundred."

Shirley fidgeted with the hem of her habit. Margaret, undeterred, tilted her head and smiled sweetly. "Perhaps there's been a... clerical error."

Marie's eyes narrowed. "A clerical error? One that conveniently results in you two receiving new shoes, a better coffee machine, and a weekend trip to Niagara Falls?"

Shirley tried to hide her feet under her chair. "They were on sale," she muttered.

Undercover Nuns

Margaret attempted to salvage the situation. "Mother Superior, surely our dedication to the parish speaks for itself. We merely... borrowed a small portion of the funds, with every intention of—"

"Borrowed?" Marie interrupted, her voice sharp enough to slice through stone. "You've turned charity into a con. I will not allow St. Peter's to become a den of thieves."

The room fell silent. Even Margaret had the sense to shut her mouth.

After a long, tense pause, Mother Superior sighed. "You've left me with no choice. Effective immediately, you are both relieved of your duties here at St. Peter's."

Shirley's jaw dropped. "You're kicking us out?"

"I am sending you out," Marie corrected. "If you're so eager to manipulate people, then perhaps you should take your talents to the streets. Go into the community. Spread the good word of God. And if you have any conscience left, perhaps you will learn the value of honesty."

Margaret stood slowly, adjusting her habit. "So... we're free agents now?"

"You're sinners in need of redemption," Marie snapped. "Leave, before I call the bishop."

Undercover Nuns

The next morning, Margaret and Shirley were unceremoniously escorted out of St. Peter's, their worldly belongings stuffed into a battered suitcase and a pair of grocery bags. They stood on the church steps, the city stretching before them.

Shirley looked uncertain. "What do we do now?"

Margaret grinned, pulling a cigarette from her sleeve. She lit it with the confidence of a woman who'd never let a small thing like being expelled from the church ruin her day. "What we do best, Shirley. We improvise."

"Mother Superior said to spread the good word."

Margaret blew a smoke ring. "Sure. And maybe make a little money on the side. You know, for the 'orphans.'" She winked.

Shirley hesitated. "We... we're not really going to steal again, are we?"

Margaret threw an arm around her friend's shoulder. "Shirley, sweetheart, we're not stealing. We're... redistributing wealth. Robin Hood, but in habits."

Their first target was a small farmers' market on the edge of city. Margaret set up a booth with a hastily painted sign: HOLY WATER – HEALS SOULS & ACHES – $5 A BOTTLE.

Shirley, dressed in full habit, held up bottles of tap water with a smile that could disarm even the most skeptical farmer.

"It's been blessed by Father Maloney himself," Shirley would say, while Margaret whispered, "Rest his soul, he's very busy these days," (conveniently leaving out that Father Maloney was alive and kicking).

Within an hour, they'd sold every bottle.

"This is too easy," Margaret said, counting the cash behind the stall. "We're practically saints."

But not everyone was convinced. A burly man with a crooked nose and a leather jacket approached their booth, holding one of their bottles. "This stuff better work," he growled. "Or I'll find you."

Margaret smiled sweetly. "Oh, it'll work wonders. Just... drink responsibly."

The man walked off, but Shirley shivered. "He looked... scary."

"Relax," Margaret said, tucking the cash into her bag. "What's the worst that could happen?"

That night, they stayed at a cheap roadside motel. Shirley sat on the edge of the bed, nervously twisting her rosary. "Margaret...

Undercover Nuns

what if Mother Superior was right? Maybe we should just... do good deeds. For real."

Margaret flopped down on the bed with a laugh. "Shirley, we are doing good deeds. Think of all those farmers. We gave them hope."

"We gave them tap water."

"Hope and hydration."

Before Shirley could argue further, there was a loud knock on the door. Margaret peeked through the curtain and cursed under her breath. "It's leather-jacket guy."

Shirley's eyes widened. "What does he want?"

Margaret whispered, "Probably a refund. Or our heads. Either way, pack your bag."

The man banged on the door. "I know you're in there, nuns! You think you can scam us?"

Shirley panicked. "Us? Who's 'us? He's got friends?"

"Mob friends," Margaret muttered, grabbing the suitcase. "We might've just sold tap water to someone connected to the local mob. Time to go."

They slipped out the bathroom window just as the door cracked under the man's fist. Running through the alley behind the motel, their habits flapping like blue wings, they didn't stop until they reached a bus station.

"Where do we go?" Shirley asked, gasping for breath.

"Anywhere but here," Margaret said, tossing cash at the ticket counter. "Two tickets. Next bus out."

As the bus rolled out of the city, Margaret grinned. "Well, Shirley, looks like we're officially out in the community, just like Mother Superior wanted."

Shirley gave her a worried glance. "Yeah, but I don't think this is what she had in mind."

Margaret leaned back, closing her eyes. "Relax. A couple of nuns on the run? What's the worst that could happen?"

Chapter 2

Sisters of Sin & Sparkle

The morning sun rose over Ottawa's outskirts, painting the city's worn streets with streaks of orange and pink. The bus from the night before rattled into a grimy station on the edge of downtown, and two unlikely passengers—Sister Margaret and Sister Shirley—stepped off with a suitcase, a bag of mismatched "holy water" bottles, and the kind of determination only desperation can provide.

Margaret adjusted her habit and surveyed the area like a general on the battlefield. "Well, Shirley, this is it. A new city. A fresh start. No Mother Superior breathing down our necks. No parishioners asking annoying questions like, 'Where's my donation going?'" She grinned. "We're free."

Shirley wasn't so sure. "We're also broke. We spent almost everything on bus tickets and those gas station sandwiches."

Margaret's grin didn't falter. "A minor detail. We'll earn more. You and me, Shirley—two sisters of the cloth, armed with charm, wit, and possibly divine intervention. How can we fail?"

Undercover Nuns

Shirley sighed, clutching her rosary like a lifeline. "Margaret... maybe we should just find another parish. Somewhere we can be... good. Like Mother Superior wanted."

Margaret chuckled. "Shirley, good doesn't pay the bills. Besides, look at this city! It's practically begging for a little 'holy guidance.' And I've got just the plan."

By noon, they had set up a makeshift booth at the city's busiest corner—a rickety card table they "borrowed" from behind a diner, covered with a white tablecloth (which was actually one of their bedsheets). A hand-painted sign read: HOLY BLESSINGS – $10 PER MIRACLE

Shirley nervously adjusted the sign. "Margaret... people are going to see right through this."

Margaret placed a hand over her heart, feigning innocence. "Shirley, I am simply providing a service. Hope. Healing. And maybe a small profit. Besides, you're the perfect pitch nun. Flash them that sweet smile, and they'll line up."

The first customer was a frazzled young mother pushing a stroller. "A miracle, you say?" she asked skeptically.

Margaret clasped her hands together. "Absolutely. For a modest donation of ten dollars, I will personally bless you, your child, and your future. Guaranteed good luck for seven days."

The woman hesitated, but Shirley stepped in with wide, soulful eyes. "It's true. I've seen Sister Margaret's blessings bring light to even the darkest hearts. Just last week, a man found his lost dog—after she blessed him."

The woman handed over a ten-dollar bill.

Margaret made an exaggerated sign of the cross, muttered something vaguely Latin (it was actually the menu from Riverside pizza), and sprinkled a few drops of "holy water" on the baby's stroller.

The woman smiled, oddly comforted. "Thank you, sisters. God bless you."

"God bless your wallet," Margaret whispered under her breath, pocketing the cash.

By late afternoon, the sisters had expanded their menu of services. A handwritten board displayed:

- Miracle Water – $5
- Personal Blessing – $10
- Cursed Neighbor Removal (Spiritual) – $20

Business was surprisingly brisk. People seemed willing to pay for anything that gave them a sliver of hope, even if that hope came in the form of two suspiciously cheeky nuns.

Undercover Nuns

"Twenty bucks for telling Mrs. Fletcher's neighbor to move her trash cans? That's a record," Margaret said, counting the day's earnings.

Shirley looked conflicted. "Do you ever feel... guilty?"

Margaret smirked. "Of course not. We're giving people what they want—comfort, hope, and a good story to tell their friends. It's practically charity."

"Charity that involves stealing."

"Borrowing with style," Margaret corrected.

Just as they were about to close up, a man approached their booth. He was tall, broad-shouldered, and dressed in a dark suit. His hair was slicked back, and his sharp eyes glinted like knives. A gold chain hung around his neck, and his knuckles bore several heavy rings.

"Ladies," he said, his voice smooth but menacing. "I hear you're in the blessing business."

Margaret gave her brightest smile. "Indeed, sir. Are you looking for a miracle?"

The man smirked. "You could say that. Name's Tony. I work for some... important people around here. People who like to stay lucky if you catch my drift."

Shirley's eyes widened. "Lucky?"

Tony leaned on the table. "I'll give you five hundred dollars if you bless something for me."

Margaret's ears practically perked up like a dog hearing the word "treat." "Five hundred? What needs blessing?"

Tony pulled out a velvet pouch and set it on the table. He loosened the strings and revealed a cluster of sparkling, cut diamonds. "These," he said softly. "My bosses just acquired them. We need them blessed. For... good luck."

Shirley stammered, "D-diamonds? Real diamonds?"

Margaret, ever composed, nodded. "Of course. Blessing valuables is one of our specialties."

Margaret whispered to Shirley as Tony stepped aside to take a phone call. "These are worth a fortune."

"Boss - Yes, I have got them. They are currently being blessed by two nuns. Ya, we can trust them. They are nuns, Tony said."

Shirley's voice trembled. "Margaret... that guy looks dangerous. We can't mess with him."

Undercover Nuns

"Shirley, this is divine providence. God sent us these diamonds for a reason."

"Stealing is not a reason!"

Margaret ignored her and picked up the pouch. She waved her hands over the diamonds and recited what sounded like a blessing but was, in fact, the recipe for her grandmother's stew. Then, in a smooth motion, she swapped the pouch with one of their holy water bottles, which she had filled earlier with cheap rhinestones bought from a thrift shop.

Tony returned, unaware of the switch. "Is it done?"

Margaret handed him the fake pouch with a solemn nod. "They are blessed. Fortune will follow you."

Tony smiled and dropped a stack of bills on the table. "Thanks. Pleasure doing business, sisters."

As soon as he was gone, Shirley gasped. "Margaret... you just ripped off the mob!"

Margaret grinned, holding the real diamonds like they were relics of the saints. "Sister, I think we've just been promoted."

That night, they rented a room at a slightly nicer motel, their suitcase now holding both cash and diamonds. Shirley paced the room. "Margaret, this is insane. That guy is going to find out. They'll kill us!"

"Relax," Margaret said, lounging on the bed. "By the time Tony figures it out, we'll be kilometers away. We're not amateurs, Shirley. We're professionals now."

"Professionals? We're nuns!"

"Former nuns," Margaret corrected. "And besides, we're still spreading the good word— 'Don't mess with Sister Margaret.'"

Shirley collapsed onto the chair, muttering prayers under her breath.

Around midnight, a loud knock rattled their door. Margaret froze. "You expecting room service?"

Shirley's face went pale. "It's them. They've found us."

Margaret motioned for her to stay quiet. She peeked through the peephole. A shadowy figure stood outside, tapping something metallic against the doorframe.

"Ladies," a voice called. "We need to talk."

Margaret's mind raced. "Pack the bag. We're leaving."

Undercover Nuns

Shirley whispered, "How? He's right outside!"

Margaret opened the bathroom window.
"Through the back. Again."

They bolted from the motel, diamonds, and cash
in tow, just as the door splintered behind them.
Shirley tripped over her habit but scrambled to
her feet, her heart pounding. They sprinted
through alleys, past dumpsters, and barking
dogs, until they found themselves in an
industrial area.

Margaret bent over, catching her breath.
"Okay... new plan. We lay low for a bit. Then we
find someone to... unload these diamonds."

Shirley's eyes widened. "You mean sell them?"

"What did you think, I'd make a diamond-
encrusted rosary? Of course we'll sell them."

"But to who? We can't exactly walk into a pawn
shop in our habits!"

Margaret smirked. "Leave that to me."

The next morning, they hid out in a café,
sipping coffee and plotting their next move. A
TV mounted in the corner blared the news:

"Local Authorities Warn of Mob Activity:
Diamond Heist Suspected."

Shirley's jaw dropped. "That's... that's them. That's Tony's crew."

Margaret grinned, spinning her coffee spoon. "And now, they're going to be looking for whoever has their shiny little trinkets. Guess we'll have to be extra clever."

"Margaret... this is going to end badly."

Margaret's smile widened. "Or it's going to end fabulously. Imagine it, Shirley. We take this money, sell the diamonds, and retire on a beach somewhere. Margaritas, not confessionals."

Shirley groaned. "We're going to hell."

Margaret raised her cup. "At least we'll go in style."

Chapter 3

Sins, Stones, & Sirens

By the next morning, Margaret and Shirley were running on adrenaline and bad motel coffee. They had the diamonds stuffed inside a hollowed-out Bible—a trick Margaret claimed she'd learned from a "particularly creative" altar boy. The problem wasn't hiding them. The problem was unloading them without ending up at the bottom of the Ottawa River wearing cement shoes.

Shirley sat cross-legged on the bed, the Bible open in her lap. The diamonds sparkled in the weak morning light. "These things are cursed," she said, half-whispering as if the stones themselves could hear. "I can feel it. They're going to get us killed."

Margaret, leaning against the dresser while smoking, waved her hand dismissively. "Cursed? Please. These are a blessing—literally delivered into our hands. We're talking enough money to buy a villa in Italy. Or at least a condo in Calgary."

Shirley gave her a sharp look. "Margaret... we *stole* from the mob."

"We didn't *steal*," Margaret corrected with a grin. "We... facilitated an unapproved transfer of assets. There's a difference."

Shirley closed the Bible with a snap. "Tony's going to find us. You saw that guy—he looks like he flosses with barbed wire."

Margaret smirked. "Then we don't stick around long enough for him to find us. We need someone who can move these diamonds fast."

By mid-afternoon, Margaret had a plan. "There's a place downtown," she said, leading Shirley through a maze of graffiti-smeared alleys. "Eddie's Pawn & Collectibles. He's not picky about where things come from. We'll just say these diamonds were a donation from a 'generous parishioner.'"

Shirley crossed herself. "I'm pretty sure lying about parishioners is a fast track to eternal damnation."

Margaret shrugged. "So is smoking, drinking, and yelling at choir kids, but you don't see me sweating the small stuff."

They arrived at Eddie's—a dingy shop with a flickering neon sign that read WE BUY ANYTHING. The interior smelled faintly of old leather and bad decisions. Eddie, a wiry man with glasses perched on the end of his nose, looked up from behind the counter.

"Well, well," he said, eyeing their habits. "Two sisters from the church. Haven't seen your kind in here before. What can I do for you?"

Margaret set the Bible on the counter and opened it with a flourish. "We've come into possession of some... heavenly stones."

Eddie's eyes widened at the sight of the diamonds. "Where in God's name did you get these?"

Margaret smiled sweetly. "Let's just say they were a donation from a very pious fellow who wanted to... secure a place in heaven."

Eddie wasn't convinced. "These aren't just rocks, ladies. These are high-grade diamonds. And from the looks of them, I'd say someone *very dangerous* is missing them."

Shirley swallowed hard. "See, Margaret? He knows."

Margaret leaned closer to Eddie, her tone dropping to a whisper. "How much?"

Eddie sighed, rubbing his temples. "Look, I don't want trouble with whoever you ripped off. But if you're serious, I can find a buyer. Might take a day or two."

Margaret shook her head. "We don't have a day or two. Tony is probably already looking for us."

Eddie froze. "Tony? Tony Marino?"

Shirley gasped. "You know him?"

"Know him?" Eddie laughed nervously. "Everyone in this city knows Tony. He runs half the underground. If he finds out I'm involved..." He shook his head. "Forget it. I'm out."

Unfortunately for the sisters, Tony Marino was already sniffing around. Back at his office—a smoky bar in the basement of a strip mall—he stood with his crew, holding the fake rhinestones Margaret had handed him the day before.

"This is what they gave me?" Tony roared, slamming the pouch on the table. "Plastic. Freakin' plastic."

One of his men, Vinny, scratched his head. "Boss, they're nuns. Who scams a nun?"

Tony glared. "These aren't nuns. These are wolves in habits. And I'm gonna find them."

He tossed a photo on the table—grainy security footage from a convenience store, showing Margaret and Shirley laughing as they bought snacks. "They're in the city. Track them. Start with pawn shops. Someone's gotta move those rocks."

Undercover Nuns

Back at Eddie's shop, Margaret was still trying to negotiate. "Come on, Eddie. We'll give you a cut. Forty percent."

"Fifty," Eddie countered. "And I want no part in it if Tony shows up."

"Deal," Margaret said instantly.

Shirley, wringing her hands, whispered, "Margaret, maybe we should just return them."

Margaret shot her a look. "And apologize to Tony? What are we, lunatics?"

Before Shirley could respond, the bell above the door chimed. In walked a man in a black leather jacket—one of Tony's crew. His eyes immediately swept the store.

Margaret's pulse spiked. "Time to leave."

She grabbed Shirley by the arm and shoved the diamonds back into the Bible. "Bless you, Eddie," she said, yanking her friend toward the back door.

The thug spotted them. "Hey! You two!"

They bolted.

The chase spilled into the alley behind Eddie's. Margaret yanked off her habit veil to move faster, while Shirley hiked up her skirt, nearly tripping over herself. The thug pursued, shouting into a phone. "Yeah, I found them! They got the stones!"

Margaret grabbed a trash can lid and tossed it behind her like a shield, smacking the thug in the shin. "Sorry! Blessings be upon you!"

They darted through side streets, weaving between parked cars and honking traffic, until they finally ducked into an abandoned warehouse. Shirley collapsed against a wall, gasping.

"This is insane," she wheezed. "We're being hunted by the mob. We're going to die in these habits."

Margaret grinned, even as she panted. "Not today, sister. Not today."

Once they caught their breath, Margaret came up with another plan. "We need allies. Someone who hates the mob as much as we do."

Shirley stared. "We don't hate the mob. We're just trying to stay alive!"

Margaret ignored her. "The cops. They're always trying to take down guys like Tony, right? Maybe we can trade information for protection."

Shirley groaned. "Margaret... we stole from the mob. You think the cops are going to give us a medal?"

"Not unless we give them something bigger. We'll hand over the mob's operations... and keep the diamonds."

Shirley's jaw dropped. "You're insane lady."

Margaret winked. "I'm resourceful."

That night, as they tried to sleep in the warehouse, the sound of tires screeching outside jolted them awake. Shirley peeked through a crack in the door. "Margaret... it's them. Tony's guys. They're outside."

Margaret grabbed the Bible. "Then it's time for Plan B."

"Which is?"

"Run. Again."

As they sprinted into the night, sirens suddenly wailed down the street. A black SUV with RCMP MOB DIVISION stenciled on the side screeched to a stop. Out stepped Detective Louie Laframboise, a tall, no-nonsense officer with a trimmed beard and a look that could freeze lava.

"You two," he barked, holding up his badge. "Stop right there."

Margaret froze mid-step. "Are you arresting us or saving us?"

"Depends," Laframboise said. "What's in the Bible?"

Shirley stammered. "Um... Scripture?"

Margaret grinned. "And a few... precious blessings."

Undercover Nuns

Laframboise's gaze hardened. "Get in the car. Now. Before the mob gets here."

Margaret raised an eyebrow. "Are we under arrest?"

"Not yet," Laframboise said, glancing over his shoulder as headlights appeared at the end of the street. "But if you want to live, you'll come with me."

The sisters climbed into the back of the RCMP vehicle as Tony's men rounded the corner. Margaret smirked at Shirley. "See? We're moving up in the world. First, we rip off the mob. Now, we're riding with the Mounties."

Shirley groaned. "This is not a promotion. This is a death sentence."

Margaret chuckled as the SUV sped off into the night. "Sister, have a little faith."

Chapter 4

Habits & Handcuffs

Detective Laframboise drove with one hand on the wheel, his eyes flicking between the road and the rearview mirror. The SUV tore through the quiet streets, leaving Tony's men and their black sedans behind. Margaret and Shirley sat in the back seat, wide-eyed, clutching the Bible that held their ill-gotten diamonds.

"You two have a lot of explaining to do," Laframboise said, his tone sharp and controlled.

Margaret crossed her arms and leaned back. "You first, Detective. What exactly is the RCMP Mob Division doing rescuing two harmless nuns?"

"Harmless?" Laframboise scoffed, glancing at them through the mirror. "You've managed to piss off Tony Marino, the most dangerous mob boss in this province. That's not harmless. That's suicidal."

Shirley gulped. "We didn't mean to. We just... blessed his diamonds."

"Blessed?" Laframboise said, his voice rising. "Do you have any idea what kind of operation you've stumbled into? Those diamonds were part of a massive heist Tony's crew pulled last month. Millions in stolen goods. Now he's gunning for anyone who touches them."

Margaret's smirk didn't falter. "So, you're saying we accidentally robbed the mob?"

"Accidentally or not," Laframboise said, "you're in over your heads. And now you're a liability— both to the mob and to my investigation."

Shirley clutched the Bible tighter. "We didn't ask for any of this! We just... left the church to spread the good word."

Laframboise shot her a look. "The good word? More like the *bad hustle*. I know your type. You think those habits make you untouchable, but you're con artists. Am I wrong?"

Margaret raised an eyebrow. "Detective, I prefer the term 'creative fundraisers.'"

Laframboise sighed. "Here's the deal. You either work with me to bring down Tony's operation, or I haul you in right now for obstruction, theft, and fraud. Your choice."

Shirley's jaw dropped. "We can't work with the police! We're nuns!"

"Ex-nuns," Laframboise corrected. "And trust me, the alternative is a lot worse. Tony Marino doesn't do forgiveness."

Margaret leaned forward, her grin returning. "What's in it for us?"

Laframboise's jaw tightened. "Protection. You help me get Tony, and I make sure you don't end up floating in the Ottawa River."

Margaret smirked. "Do we get to keep the diamonds?"

"No," Laframboise said flatly.

Margaret sighed. "Fine. But I want to ride shotgun."

While Laframboise drove them to an RCMP safe house, Tony Marino and his men gathered in their hideout. Tony paced the floor, cigar smoke curling around his head. Vinny, his right-hand man, leaned against the wall, nervously cracking his knuckles.

"You find them yet?" Tony barked.

"Not yet, boss," Vinny said. "But we got a lead. Someone saw 'em running with a Mountie."

Tony's eyes narrowed. "The RCMP's involved? That means those sisters are trouble. I want them found. No excuses."

"What about the diamonds?" Vinny asked.

Tony slammed his fist on the table. "We get the diamonds back, and then we deal with the holy hustlers. Nobody rips off Tony Marino and lives to tell the tale."

The safe house was a nondescript bungalow on the outskirts of the city. Laframboise parked the SUV and led the sisters inside. The interior was plain—beige walls, cheap furniture, and a faint smell of stale coffee. It looked nothing like the cozy parish they were used to.

Shirley looked around nervously. "This is... safe?"

Laframboise locked the door behind them. "For now. But if Tony's men catch wind of you, even this place won't hold."

Margaret plopped down on the couch, tossing her habit over the armrest. "Well, Detective, since we're on the same team now, what's the plan? I assume you don't just want us sitting here praying for divine intervention."

"You're going to help me get close to Tony," Laframboise said. "Your scam with the blessings gave you an in. If we can convince him that you're back to make amends, we can gather intel on his diamond operation."

Shirley's eyes widened. "You want us to go *back* to him? Are you insane?"

Laframboise shrugged. "You're the only ones who can pull it off. He already knows your faces. With my team watching, you'll be safe."

Margaret grinned. "I like the sound of this. Undercover nuns. Has a nice ring to it, doesn't it?"

Shirley groaned. "This is going to end with us in confession for the next fifty years."

The next day, Laframboise put the sisters through what he called "basic undercover training." This mostly involved teaching them how to wear wires, how to avoid getting shot, and how not to accidentally incriminate themselves.

Undercover Nuns

Margaret excelled. She strutted around the living room with the confidence of a professional spy, practicing her "innocent nun" act while secretly recording conversations.

Shirley, on the other hand, was a disaster. She fumbled with the microphone, dropped the transmitter in her coffee, and at one point asked if lying to the mob counted as a sin.

"Yes," Laframboise said, pinching the bridge of his nose. "But so does getting killed, so maybe just focus on staying alive."

Meanwhile, Tony's crew had set up an ambush. They'd spread word throughout the city that Tony was "looking to forgive" the sisters if they returned what they'd taken. It was a trap, of course, but Tony knew their type. He was counting on greed—or stupidity—bringing them back.

"They'll come crawling," Tony said with a grin, flipping one of the fake rhinestones between his fingers. "And when they do, we'll make an example out of them."

Laframboise's team intercepted the rumor before the sisters heard it. "Tony's baiting you," he told them. "This is perfect. We'll let him think you're taking the bait, and we'll be there to shut it down."

Shirley looked horrified. "You want us to walk into a mob trap on purpose?"

"Yes," Laframboise said. "But don't worry. We'll be in position the whole time."

Margaret smirked. "This is starting to feel like one of those action movies. Do I get a cool code name?"

"No," Laframboise said. "You're still just 'Sister Margaret.'"

The night of the operation, the sisters dressed in their habits again, but Laframboise insisted on a few modifications. Shirley's rosary had a hidden camera in the cross. Margaret's habit had a microphone sewn into the hem.

Margaret twirled in front of the mirror. "I have to admit, this is the best I've ever looked."

"You look like trouble," Shirley muttered. "The kind that ends with cement shoes."

Margaret grinned. "That's what makes it fun."

Chapter 5

Diamonds & Divine Disasters

The rendezvous point was a dimly lit warehouse near the docks—a classic mob hangout, complete with broken windows and the faint smell of gasoline. Laframboise's team was stationed nearby in unmarked cars, ready to move in.

They entered as if they were the proprietors of the establishment. She sensed Shirley quaking next to her, the beads of her rosary rattling anxiously like wind chimes caught in a tempest. Tony Marino was positioned at the heart of the concrete expanse, flanked by two of his henchmen: Vinny, the one with the bent nose, and a massive individual who appeared capable of crushing coconuts with his bare hands.

"Well, well," Tony drawled, his voice low and dangerous. "The holy sisters have returned to bless us with their presence. How thoughtful."

Margaret flashed her best sweet-nun smile. "Tony, darling, I know there's been... a misunderstanding. We only wanted to bring you good fortune."

Tony's grin was humorless. "Good fortune? You swapped my diamonds for cheap rhinestones.

Undercover Nuns

Do I look like I need a joke from a nun? Where are my diamonds?"

Margaret kept smiling, but her pulse was pounding in her ears. "What can I say? God works in mysterious ways. We have them."

Tony gestured to Vinny, who stepped forward with a sneer. "Search 'em."

As Vinny approached, Shirley's panic escalated. "Margaret," she whispered, "they're going to find the wire."

Margaret whispered back, "Keep calm. Act holy."

Shirley tried. She closed her eyes, muttering what sounded like a prayer. Vinny stopped in front of her and gave her a once-over. "What's this?" He tugged at the rosary around her neck.

"It's... it's my sacred beads," Shirley stammered. "For prayer."

Vinny squinted at the tiny camera embedded in the cross. "This looks... expensive."

Margaret stepped in smoothly. "It's a gift from the Vatican. Very exclusive. If you break it, you're offending the Pope himself."

Undercover Nuns

Vinny hesitated, looking at Tony. Tony waved him off. "Fine. But if you're lying, sister, you'll regret it."

Shirley exhaled shakily as Vinny backed away.

"Please hand over the diamonds, sister," Margaret instructed. Shirley reached into the hollowed-out Bible and handed him the bag.

"Thank you," Tony replied.

Meanwhile, Detective Laframboise and his RCMP team were stationed outside in unmarked vehicles, listening to every word through Margaret's concealed microphone.

"Keep them talking," Laframboise muttered, adjusting his earpiece. "We need confirmation of the new shipment of diamonds before we move."

Through the wire, they heard Tony say, "You want forgiveness? Then you're going to help me."

"Help you?" Margaret asked cautiously.

Tony nodded. "There's a shipment coming in tonight. More diamonds. You're going to bless it, make sure it goes smooth. And if you screw it up again..." He made a cutting gesture across his throat. "You won't get another chance."

Laframboise's voice came through Margaret's earpiece. "We need them to play along. We'll bust the operation when the diamonds change hands."

Margaret responded softly under her breath. "Copy that. But if I end up in the Ottawa River, I'm haunting you, Laframboise."

Margaret clapped her hands together. "Tony, consider it done. We'll bless your shipment. God loves a good diamond, after all."

Shirley hissed, "Margaret!"

Tony smirked. "Good. You've got about four hours. And don't even think of double crossing me again."

Margaret nodded. "Four hours. Easy."

As Tony's men escorted them out of the warehouse, Shirley muttered, "We're going to die. I can feel it."

Margaret grinned. "Relax, sister. This is all part of the plan."

Back in Laframboise's SUV, the sisters were debriefed while the detective laid out his strategy.

"The diamonds are coming in by boat tonight," Laframboise explained. "We'll be stationed at the docks. You two will bless the shipment as planned, and while Tony's distracted, we'll swoop in and arrest him and his crew."

"Sounds simple," Margaret said, leaning back with her arms crossed. "Which means it's going to be a disaster."

Shirley raised her hand nervously. "Um... what if the mob figures out, we're working with you?"

Laframboise gave her a dry look. "Then I suggest you run faster than you did last time."

Undercover Nuns

The docks were cold and foggy that night, the water black and still under the moonlight. Tony's men were already there, unloading crates from a sleek speedboat. Margaret and Shirley, dressed in their habits, walked toward the scene as if they were simply arriving for Sunday mass.

"Ah, the sisters," Tony said, his voice echoing over the water. "Time for some divine intervention."

Margaret stepped forward with her usual flair. "Of course, Tony. Let's bless these jewels so they sparkle with the light of heaven."

As she pretended to sprinkle holy water, she whispered into her wire. "Laframboise, they're here. Lots of them. I count at least seven men."

"Hold position," Laframboise's voice crackled in her ear. "We're moving in."

Just as the RCMP team prepared to strike, one of Tony's men noticed something odd. He pointed at Shirley's rosary, which had started blinking faintly due to a low battery on the camera.

"Hey," the man said, squinting. "What's that light?"

Shirley froze. "Oh, that's... divine energy. A sign from above."

Undercover Nuns

The man didn't buy it. "Looks like a camera to me."

Tony's eyes darkened. "Camera?"

Before anyone could react, Margaret grabbed a crate and tipped it over, spilling diamonds across the dock. "Look! Divine blessings all over the place!" she shouted.

The distraction worked for about two seconds—just enough time for Laframboise and his team to storm in.

"RCMP! Drop your weapons!" Laframboise bellowed as his team swarmed the docks. Flashlights cut through the fog, and the sound of boots pounding against wood echoed like a drumroll.

Tony cursed, pulling a pistol from his jacket. "You set me up!" he shouted at the sisters.

Shirley screamed. "It wasn't me! I swear!"

Margaret grabbed Shirley by the arm and ducked behind a stack of crates as bullets and shouts filled the night air. Laframboise's officers engaged with Tony's crew, and chaos erupted.

In the middle of the chaos, Margaret spotted the spilled diamonds glittering on the dock. "Opportunity knocks, sister," she whispered, scooping up as many as she could into her habit.

"Margaret!" Shirley gasped. "We're supposed to help the police, not steal from *both* sides!"

"Think of it as a retirement plan," Margaret said, stuffing another handful into her pocket.

As the RCMP subdued the last of Tony's men, Laframboise spotted the sisters sneaking toward the parking lot. "Hey! Where do you think you're going?"

"Confession!" Margaret shouted over her shoulder.

Laframboise groaned. "You're unbelievable."

By dawn, Tony Marino was in custody, his operation severely crippled. Laframboise, exhausted but victorious, called a team meeting at the safe house.

"You two are lucky," he told the sisters. "If it weren't for your help—accidental as it was— Tony would still be out there."

Shirley smiled nervously. "So... we're free to go?"

Laframboise narrowed his eyes. "For now. But if you pull another stunt like that—especially with

Undercover Nuns

those diamonds—I'll personally drag you back here."

Margaret grinned. "Oh, Detective, you worry too much. We're just two innocent sisters trying to find our path."

Laframboise muttered something under his breath that sounded like, "Yeah, right."

Chapter 6

Blessed & Bugged

Detective Laframboise was not the type to lose his temper easily, but dealing with Sister Margaret and Sister Shirley had pushed him close to the brink. He rubbed his temples as the two nuns sat across from him at the RCMP safe house kitchen table, sipping coffee like they had just returned from a spa rather than a mob bust.

Undercover Nuns

"You do realize," Laframboise began, his voice slow and deliberate, "that you nearly got *all of us* killed tonight?"

Margaret raised an eyebrow, feigning innocence. "Detective, I think 'killed' is a bit dramatic. We were in *very* capable hands. Besides, we helped catch Tony, didn't we?"

"You also stole half the diamonds from the scene," Laframboise said flatly.

Shirley's jaw dropped. "Margaret! You didn't—"

"They were just lying there," Margaret said with a shrug. "Like God Himself was telling me to pick them up. I call that divine opportunity."

Laframboise pinched the bridge of his nose. "Where are they?"

Margaret smiled sweetly. "Safe."

"Return. The. Diamonds." Laframboise's tone left no room for argument.

Margaret sighed. "Fine. But you owe us one."

With Tony Marino in custody, Laframboise expected things to calm down. They didn't. Within twenty-four hours, intelligence revealed that Tony's crew wasn't the only mob element involved in the diamond smuggling ring. A bigger, more dangerous player—known only as *The Viper*—was orchestrating the heist from the shadows.

"We need someone on the inside," Laframboise told his team. "Someone they wouldn't suspect."

Shirley paled. "You're not thinking—"

Laframboise smirked. "Oh, I am. Margaret, Shirley... congratulations. You're going deep undercover."

Margaret's eyes lit up like Christmas lights. "Finally! I knew I was destined for undercover work."

Shirley groaned. "I'm going to die in a habit."

Laframboise arranged for a cover story that was both absurd and plausible. Margaret and Shirley would pose as "blessing consultants"—spiritual advisors who specialized in bringing luck to high-stakes deals. With Tony's crew dismantled, The Viper's syndicate was reportedly looking for a "lucky charm" to bless an upcoming diamond exchange.

"You'll play the part of holy women who can guarantee safe deals," Laframboise explained. "We'll feed you intel through the wire. Your job is to get close enough to gather evidence."

Margaret grinned. "Sounds like a con. I'm in."

Shirley wrung her hands. "Why do I always get dragged into your terrible ideas?"

"Because you love me," Margaret said with a wink.

"How will we determine the identity of the Viper?" Margaret inquired. "I have Tony's phone. The contact is saved as V - it must be him. We will arrange for someone to alter their voice and impersonate Tony, convincing him to trust you and Shirley to bless their shipment of diamonds," Laframboise clarified.

Two days later, Margaret and Shirley—fully dressed in their crisp blue-and-white habits—were escorted by Laframboise into a high-end lounge downtown, the kind of place where the liquor cost more than their monthly budget back at St. Peter's.

A man with slicked-back hair and a three-piece suit approached them. His sharp eyes scanned them from head to toe. "You're the nuns Tony mentioned?"

Margaret smiled and stepped forward. "Indeed. I'm Sister Margaret, and this is Sister Shirley. We specialize in... divine consultations."

The man arched a brow. "The Viper doesn't trust many outsiders. You two better be worth it."

Margaret leaned in, lowering her voice like she was sharing a secret. "Luck tends to follow those who believe. And with us, luck isn't a maybe—it's a guarantee."

Shirley nodded nervously. "We're very... blessed."

They were led into a private room where a tall, thin man in a dark green suit waited. His face was partially hidden by the shadows, but his voice was smooth and chilling. "So, these are the sisters Tony vouched for," The Viper said.

Margaret dipped her head slightly. "At your service."

The Viper studied them for a moment before smirking. "Tony said you two were... unconventional. I like unconventional. But I don't like mistakes. Can you guarantee that our next shipment arrives safely?"

Margaret, never missing a beat, smiled. "With our blessings, not even the devil himself could interfere."

Shirley whispered, "Why would you even say that?"

Through the hidden microphone sewn into Margaret's sleeve, Laframboise's voice crackled softly in her ear. "*Stay calm. Get details on the shipment location and timing. Don't push too hard.*"

Margaret muttered under her breath, "Relax, Detective. I've got this."

Shirley glanced at her nervously. "You're talking to yourself again."

The Viper tilted his head. "Problem?"

Margaret smiled sweetly. "Just praying."

Over the next hour, Margaret and Shirley managed to charm The Viper with a mix of "blessings" and shameless theatrics. Margaret sprinkled holy water over his briefcase, muttering a fake Latin prayer, while Shirley handed out small crosses she'd bought at a dollar store.

The Viper chuckled. "You two are... amusing. I like that. Maybe you'll bring me the luck I need."

Margaret flashed a grin. "Luck is our specialty."

When The Viper finally revealed details of the next shipment—a multimillion-dollar diamond deal set to take place in a secluded warehouse on the waterfront—Laframboise's team immediately started planning a raid.

"You'll go in as part of the blessing ceremony," Laframboise explained back at the safe house. "We'll intercept the diamonds during the exchange. All you have to do is stall until we're ready."

Margaret leaned back, smirking. "Stalling is my superpower."

Shirley muttered, "So is lying."

Margaret winked. "Exactly."

Before the operation, Laframboise insisted on a few upgrades to their appearance. Their habits were subtly reinforced with lightweight Kevlar—"just in case," he said—and their rosaries were replaced with high-tech versions equipped with transmitters.

Margaret admired herself in the mirror. "Bulletproof habits. I feel like a superhero."

Shirley frowned. "I feel like we're walking into a disaster."

On the night of the exchange, the sisters arrived at the waterfront warehouse. The Viper's men were already there, unloading crates. The Viper himself stood by, overseeing every detail.

Margaret approached him with a confident smile. "Shall we begin the blessings?"

The Viper nodded. "Make it quick."

As Margaret began her "ceremony," sprinkling water and mumbling nonsense Latin phrases, Shirley noticed something troubling: one of The Viper's men was scanning the area with what looked like a signal detector.

"Margaret," Shirley whispered, "he's checking for bugs."

Margaret didn't miss a beat. She smiled and loudly proclaimed, "May the Lord bless these humble tools of commerce!"

The man's device beeped faintly as he passed near Margaret's sleeve. Her heart skipped a beat. *If he finds the mic, we're dead,* she thought.

Thinking fast, she grabbed Shirley's hand and exclaimed, "Sister Shirley, the spirits are telling me to... dance!"

"Dance?" Shirley blinked.

"Yes! A holy jitterbug dance!" Margaret twirled dramatically, moving away from the detector just as it began to spike. Shirley, flustered, tried to mimic her.

The Viper raised an eyebrow. "Is this... normal?"

"Completely," Margaret said, spinning. "The blessings are more effective if we... move with the spirit."

Margaret glanced at Shirley. "Time to make a scene," she whispered.

"How?"

Margaret grinned. "Leave that to me."

Chapter 7

Faith & Falling Diamonds

The warehouse was tense, filled with the low hum of whispered conversations and the clatter of crates being shifted. The Viper's men moved like clockwork, unloading the final shipment of diamonds. Margaret and Shirley stood in the center of the chaos, dressed in their bulletproof habits, trying their best to look like "holy advisors" while secretly plotting an escape plan that could save both their lives—and steal the diamonds.

Laframboise's voice came through the wire. "*Ladies, we're thirty seconds from go time. Just keep them distracted.*"

"Distracted?" Margaret whispered. "Darling, that's my specialty."

Shirley groaned under her breath. "This is going to end badly. I can feel it."

Margaret stepped forward, raising her hands dramatically like a preacher at a revival. "Gentlemen, before this exchange of... fine merchandise... let us ask for divine favor."

The Viper's sharp eyes narrowed slightly, but he gestured for his men to pause. "You have two minutes, Sister. Make it quick."

Margaret pulled a bottle of "holy water" (actually tap water from the safe house sink) from her sleeve. "This is no ordinary water," she declared. "This is sanctified by the prayers of saints and infused with... ah, heavenly essence."

Shirley leaned over and whispered, "Heavenly essence? You're just making stuff up."

"Shh," Margaret hissed, smiling brightly at The Viper. "Shall we begin?"

She walked to the nearest crate and sprinkled water over it, muttering a string of fake Latin phrases. "Riverside's *pizza... angelic sauce... blessed be thy pepperoni.*"

Shirley nearly choked trying not to laugh.

Margaret's fake ritual was just strange enough to keep the men entertained, but the man with the signal detector from earlier was back, sweeping the room again.

"Margaret," Shirley whispered frantically. "The detector guy! He's heading right for you!"

Undercover Nuns

Thinking quickly, Margaret clutched her stomach and fell to her knees. "Oh no! I'm receiving a holy vision!"

The Viper frowned. "A what?"

Margaret looked up with wide, dramatic eyes. "The angels are speaking to me! They say... there is treachery nearby!" She pointed vaguely toward the crates, buying time.

The men froze, glancing at each other.

Laframboise's voice came through her earpiece. *"We're going in. Brace yourselves."*

Suddenly, the warehouse doors burst open. RCMP officers stormed in, flashlights and rifles raised. "RCMP! Drop your weapons!" Laframboise's voice boomed over the commotion.

Chaos erupted. The Viper's men scrambled for cover, and gunfire echoed in the cavernous space. Margaret grabbed Shirley by the hand and ducked behind a stack of crates.

As Laframboise's team engaged the mobsters, Margaret's eyes locked on a metal briefcase lying on top of one of the crates—the diamonds. They were just sitting there, waiting for someone to grab them.

"Shirley," she whispered, "cover me."

"Cover you? With what, prayer?" Shirley hissed.

Margaret ignored her and darted across the floor, weaving between stacks of boxes as bullets flew overhead. She reached the briefcase, popped it open, and gasped at the glittering sight inside. "Oh, hello, beautiful."

Shirley peeked around the crate. "Margaret! Leave them!"

"Just borrowing!" Margaret shouted back, slamming the briefcase shut.

With the diamonds in hand, Margaret and Shirley began inching toward the exit. Laframboise spotted them mid-operation. "What the hell are you doing?!" he shouted over the chaos.

"Divine intervention!" Margaret yelled back.

Undercover Nuns

"Put the diamonds down and get behind me!" Laframboise barked.

"Don't worry, Detective! We'll keep them safe!" Margaret called, dragging Shirley with her.

Shirley groaned. "Margaret, we're literally stealing from *everyone* right now!"

Their escape route was blocked by two of The Viper's men. Thinking fast, Margaret spotted a ventilation shaft on the wall. "Up there! We'll crawl out!"

"You're insane," Shirley said, but followed anyway.

Margaret scrambled up first, pulling the vent cover loose with a screech of metal. She shoved the briefcase in ahead of her, then tried to squeeze in herself. "Hurry, Sister!"

Shirley grunted as she tried to follow, her habit snagging on a sharp edge. "I'm stuck! Margaret, I'm stuck!"

"Pull harder!"

"I *am!*" Shirley wailed.

Below them, one of The Viper's goons looked up. "Hey! They're in the vents!"

In the middle of all the chaos, the briefcase popped open, and a handful of diamonds spilled out, raining down onto the warehouse floor. One of The Viper's men dove for them, only to be tackled by an RCMP officer.

Laframboise shouted into his radio, "Secure those stones! And someone get the sisters out of there before they get killed!"

Within minutes, the RCMP team gained the upper hand. The Viper's men were disarmed and handcuffed, and the diamonds were secured—except for the few that Margaret had hidden in her sleeve.

Laframboise personally pulled the sisters out of the ventilation shaft, both covered in dust and looking like raccoons caught in a trash bin.

"I don't know how you two keep surviving," Laframboise said, shaking his head. "But next time, *do not improvise.*"

Margaret grinned sheepishly. "Detective, I was just following my instincts."

"Your instincts are criminal," Laframboise muttered.

Unfortunately, in the chaos, The Viper himself slipped away through a side exit. By the time Laframboise realized it, the mastermind behind the operation was gone.

"Great," Laframboise said through gritted teeth. "Now we have to hunt down a ghost."

Margaret, brushing dust off her habit, smiled slyly. "Maybe the sisters can help."

Later that night, the sisters sat in the safe house kitchen, sipping coffee while Laframboise paced. "You two are unpredictable, reckless, and—God help me—effective. But The Viper is still out there, and until we catch him, you're staying under my watch."

Shirley sighed. "We never asked for any of this. We just wanted to... spread the good word."

Margaret chuckled. "And maybe a little wealth."

Laframboise glared. "If you pocketed *anything* tonight, you better hand it over."

Margaret's smile widened. "Of course, Detective. Would I lie to you?"

Chapter 8

Showdown at the Cornwall Theater

Detective Laframboise paced back and forth inside the safe house living room like a man on the verge of losing his mind. His team had secured most of the diamonds from the warehouse raid, but the ringleader—the elusive Viper—had slipped away like smoke through a crack. Margaret and Shirley sat side by side on the couch, sipping coffee as if they hadn't nearly gotten themselves (and everyone else) killed just a few hours ago.

"We were *this close* to shutting down the entire operation," Laframboise muttered, holding his thumb and forefinger barely a centimetre apart. "And then... chaos. Again. Care to explain why you two tried to crawl out of a ventilation shaft with a briefcase full of diamonds?"

Margaret smirked, crossing her legs. "We were helping, Detective. Those diamonds were going to be evidence, right? We were just... collecting them."

Shirley nodded timidly. "Margaret said we were 'fast-tracking the chain of custody.'"

Laframboise glared. "You're lucky you didn't get yourselves shot. And if I find out you pocketed even *one* diamond—"

Margaret held up her hands innocently. "Detective, I'm shocked you'd accuse me of such a thing. Do I look like someone who would hide diamonds in a hollowed-out Bible?"

Laframboise's eyebrow shot up. "You literally did that two days ago."

While Laframboise argued with the sisters, The Viper was already plotting revenge. He sat in a dimly lit motel room on the edge of the city, a glass of whiskey in one hand and his phone in the other. His calm demeanor was far more terrifying than Tony Marino's bluster ever had been.

"They think they can steal from me and live?" The Viper said quietly to his lieutenant, a lean, sharp-eyed man named Richard. "First, the RCMP humiliated us. Now, those... *nuns.*"

Richard smirked. "They're not even real nuns, boss. They're hustlers. Clever, but sloppy."

The Viper's lips curled into a cold smile. "Sloppy gets you caught. But clever can be useful. We'll let them think they've won. Then we'll take back what's ours... and maybe take a little extra."

Undercover Nuns

The next day, they arrived in Cornwall. Margaret and Shirley were enjoying a rare quiet breakfast—black coffee for Margaret, chamomile tea for Shirley—when Laframboise stormed into their motel room with his phone. "We've got a problem," he said.

Margaret raised an eyebrow. "When don't we?"

"The Viper sent a message. He wants to make a deal."

Shirley paled. "A deal? What kind of deal?"

Laframboise placed Tony's phone on the table, showing a text message: 'Meet at the old Cornwall Theater tonight. Bring the nuns. We talk diamonds.'

Margaret grinned. "He wants *us*. Oh, I like this guy. He appreciates talent."

Laframboise scowled. "This isn't a game. He probably wants to kill you."

Margaret shrugged. "Or maybe he wants to hire us. We *are* very good."

That afternoon, Laframboise and his team prepped for the meeting at the old Cornwall Theater, a crumbling Art Deco building that had seen better days. "This is a setup," Laframboise said flatly. "No way The Viper shows up without backup."

Margaret tilted her head. "So, we set him up right back."

Laframboise groaned. "You're not in charge here."

"Technically, Detective, I'm the one who's already conned these guys twice," Margaret pointed out.

Shirley looked between them nervously. "Can we maybe... not double-cross anyone? Maybe just... cross once? For safety?"

Margaret patted Shirley's hand. "Oh, sweet sister, this is how we win. Double-cross the mob, double-cross the cops if we have to, and then retire somewhere tropical."

Laframboise narrowed his eyes. "You're not going anywhere with those diamonds."

Margaret smiled slyly. "We'll see."

The old Cornwall Theater was eerily quiet that night, its faded marquee spelling out half-broken words: "TONI _ _ _T: LIVE SH _ _." Laframboise stationed his team outside, ready to intervene at the first sign of trouble. Margaret and Shirley, dressed in their habits and carrying a small case (with decoy glass diamonds inside), walked into the lobby.

The Viper was waiting. He sat on a velvet armchair, looking perfectly at ease, as if the abandoned theater were his living room. "Sisters," he said with a smooth smile. "We meet again."

Margaret dipped her head slightly. "The pleasure is ours."

"I must admit," The Viper continued, "you have nerve. Stealing from Tony was one thing. But walking out of my warehouse with my diamonds? That takes... talent."

Shirley gulped. "We... we didn't mean to—"

Margaret cut in. "We like to think of it as divine inspiration."

The Viper leaned forward. "I'm a businessman, sisters. I don't hold grudges—if there's profit to

Undercover Nuns

be made. Here's my offer. You work for me. You bless my deals, you bring me luck, and in return... I let you live."

Shirley's face turned white. "Margaret... he's serious."

Margaret smiled. "I can tell. But see, here's the thing... we already have an employer."

Right on cue, Laframboise's voice came through Margaret's earpiece: *"We're ready. Stall him."*

Margaret took a deep breath. "You see, Mr. Viper, can I call you that? We're not just two holy sisters with a flair for theatrics. We're also working with the RCMP."

The Viper's smile froze. "Excuse me?"

Laframboise's team stormed through the theater doors, weapons drawn. "RCMP! Hands where we can see them!"

But The Viper was one step ahead. Before Laframboise's men could secure the area, hidden doors in the walls burst open and armed men poured into the theater. It was a standoff—RCMP on one side, The Viper's crew on the other, and Margaret and Shirley right in the middle.

"Detective Laframboise," The Viper said calmly, "you didn't really think I'd come here without a backup plan, did you?"

Laframboise gritted his teeth. "Drop your weapons, Viper. It's over."

The Viper chuckled. "On the contrary, I think it's just beginning."

Margaret, sensing things were about to explode, decided to take matters into her own hands. She reached into her habit and pulled out a small vial of "holy water" (pepper spray). "Blessings for everyone!" she yelled, spraying it in a wide arc.

Men on both sides started coughing and rubbing their eyes. In the chaos, Margaret grabbed Shirley's arm. "Run, Sister!"

Shirley yelped as Margaret dragged her toward the backstage exit, the decoy diamonds clutched under her arm.

In the confusion, Margaret spotted another metal case—one she was *sure* held the real diamonds. Without hesitation, she grabbed it and bolted. "Jackpot!" she shouted.

"Margaret!" Shirley cried. "You're stealing again!"

"Not stealing—repositioning assets!"

Undercover Nuns

As gunfire and shouts echoed in the theater, Margaret and Shirley slipped through a side door and sprinted down the alley. Laframboise's voice crackled in their earpieces. *"Where the hell are you two going?!"*

"Somewhere safe!" Margaret shouted back, though she had no idea where that was.

By the time Laframboise's team secured the theater, The Viper had escaped again, and the sisters were nowhere to be found. Laframboise cursed under his breath. "Those two are going to be the death of me."

Back at a dingy motel, Margaret counted the diamonds under the flickering light. "We are officially the luckiest nuns alive," she said, grinning.

Shirley looked horrified. "Margaret, we're not nuns anymore. We're fugitives."

Margaret leaned back on the bed, tossing a diamond in the air. "Fugitive, nun, hero, thief... I'm versatile."

Shirley buried her face in her hands. "We're going to hell."

Margaret grinned. "At least we'll go there rich."

Chapter 9

The Gospel According to Mayhem

The bells of St. Peter's Parish rang in the distance, their solemn tones echoing across Cornwall as if warning of the storm to come. Margaret and Shirley stood at the edge of the church courtyard, looking up at the familiar stone building where it had all begun. They had been exiled from these grounds just days ago, but now they had chosen it as the perfect battleground for the final showdown.

"Are you sure about this?" Shirley asked, wringing her hands. "I mean, staging a mob standoff at the parish seems like... well, blasphemy."

Margaret grinned. "Oh, sister, think of it as poetic justice. Besides, Mother Superior always said to spread the good word. We're just spreading it... *loudly*."

Shirley sighed. "More like spreading bullets."

Detective Laframboise's SUV screeched to a halt outside the parish gates. He stepped out, his face a mask of frustration. "I can't believe I'm saying this, but we're actually going through with your insane plan?"

Margaret smirked. "It's the perfect trap. The Viper wants the diamonds? Fine. We give him the diamonds—here. Then you swoop in, and everybody wins."

Laframboise crossed his arms. "Except for the part where you're in the middle of it and could get killed."

Shirley piped up, "I told her it was a bad idea. I told her! But does Margaret listen to me? Nooo."

"Relax," Margaret said, patting her friend's shoulder. "I have a plan. A *holy* plan."

The sisters and Laframboise's team spent the afternoon turning the parish into a makeshift trap. Wooden pews were moved to create barricades. The confession booth was wired with a small camera. Even the holy water fonts were filled with a special RCMP blend—half water, half pepper spray.

Margaret stood proudly in the nave, hands on her hips. "Look at this. A perfect combination of faith and firepower."

Mother Superior Marie, who had reluctantly agreed to let the RCMP use the parish for the operation, approached with a scowl. "Margaret. Shirley. You're bringing criminals to the house of God? This is beyond sacrilegious."

"Think of it as redemption," Margaret said with a sly grin. "We're catching bad guys and saving souls."

Marie narrowed her eyes. "If you survive this, you're scrubbing the parish floors for a year."

Margaret chuckled. "Deal."

By nightfall, the trap was set. The diamonds—real ones this time—sat in a metal case atop the altar, glinting under the soft glow of candlelight. Margaret and Shirley stood near the front pew, looking uncharacteristically serious.

The heavy doors of St. Peter's creaked open, and The Viper entered, flanked by six men armed with pistols and the kind of cold expressions that could freeze lava. His footsteps echoed against the stone floor.

"Ladies," The Viper said, his voice calm and deadly. "You've been very difficult to find."

Margaret smiled nervously. "Oh, we try."

The Viper's gaze shifted to the altar. "My diamonds."

Laframboise's voice crackled in Margaret's earpiece. "*Wait for my signal. We need him close to the altar before we move.*"

Margaret swallowed hard and stepped forward. "You know, Mr. Viper, these diamonds have caused a lot of trouble. Maybe it's time you reconsidered your line of work."

The Viper smirked. "Is that a sermon?"

"Consider it... a suggestion," Margaret said, trying to stall.

But The Viper wasn't interested in small talk. He motioned to his men. "Take them."

The signal came faster than expected. Laframboise's team burst through the side entrance, weapons raised. "RCMP! Drop your weapons!" he shouted.

What followed was pure chaos. Gunfire rang out, pews splintered, and the church organ gave a loud *clang* when someone stumbled against it. Margaret and Shirley dove behind the altar, clutching the case of diamonds.

"Margaret, this is insane!" Shirley cried.

"Insane but effective!" Margaret yelled back, grabbing the holy water font. "Cover me!"

She hurled the font's contents like a grenade. The mix of water and pepper spray splashed over two of The Viper's men, who dropped their weapons while clawing at their eyes.

With the chaos mounting, the sisters used whatever they could find. Shirley grabbed a large wooden cross and swung it like a baseball bat, knocking a thug into a row of pews.

"Forgive me!" she shouted mid-swing. "But also... ow!"

Margaret, meanwhile, wielded a brass candlestick like a club, smacking another goon across the knees. "You should've stayed home tonight, pal."

As the brawl continued, The Viper made a beeline for the diamonds. Margaret saw him and launched herself across the altar. They collided, and the case went skidding across the marble floor.

"Give it up, Viper!" Laframboise yelled, advancing with his team.

Undercover Nuns

But The Viper grabbed Margaret by the habit, pulling her up as a human shield. "Back off, or the sister gets it."

Shirley gasped. "Let her go, you snake!"

Margaret, never one to be outdone, smirked. "You really want to play this game with a nun?"

Then she did the unexpected—she stomped on his foot, elbowed him in the gut, and kneed him square in the groin. The Viper dropped like a rock.

"Blessed be the knees," Margaret quipped, retrieving the diamonds.

With The Viper incapacitated, Laframboise's team swept in and secured the rest of his men. Handcuffs clicked, weapons were confiscated, and the church slowly fell silent.

Laframboise approached Margaret, shaking his head. "I don't know how you do it. Every time I think you've pushed your luck too far, you somehow land on your feet."

Margaret grinned. "Faith, Detective. And maybe a little bit of charm."

Shirley sighed. "And dumb luck."

Mother Superior Marie marched down the aisle, her face red with fury. "You turned my parish into a war zone! Do you have any idea how much damage you've done?"

Margaret looked around at the broken pews and shattered windows. "Let's call it... an unorthodox form of exorcism?"

Marie glared. "You two are *still* scrubbing floors for a year."

Shirley groaned. "A year? Can we at least get hazard pay?"

As the RCMP loaded the arrested mobsters into vans outside, Margaret and Shirley sat on the church steps, watching the flashing lights.

"Think we'll ever get a normal life back?" Shirley asked.

Margaret laughed. "Normal? Sister, I think we're way past normal."

Shirley glanced at her. "What now?"

Margaret smirked. "Well, we've got a pile of trouble, a bruised mob boss, and one more chapter of life to figure out. I'd say we're just getting started."

Chapter 10

Saints, Sinners, & Second Chances

The sun rose over Cornwall, casting soft golden light through the stained-glass windows of St. Peter's Parish. The church, still littered with splintered wood and debris from the previous night's showdown, looked like a battlefield dressed up for Sunday mass. Margaret and Shirley sat side by side on the church steps, sipping lukewarm coffee as if nothing had happened.

Shirley groaned, rubbing her aching shoulders. "My arms hurt from swinging that cross. I think I've got bruises on top of bruises."

Margaret smirked. "All part of being a warrior of faith, sister. We've survived bullets, mobsters, and a very cranky Mother Superior. I'd say we're doing pretty well."

Detective Laframboise approached, his usual stern expression softened by a hint of admiration. "I'll give you this," he said, folding his arms, "you two are impossible to predict. But you helped us bring down The Viper's entire network. He's in custody, and the diamonds are now evidence in a multi-million-dollar case."

Margaret raised an eyebrow. "You're welcome."

Laframboise shook his head. "Don't push your luck."

By mid-morning, news vans crowded the street outside the parish. Headlines flashed across TV screens:

"NUNS HELP TAKE DOWN CRIME SYNDICATE."
"HOLY HEROES OR CON ARTISTS?"

Reporters clamored for interviews, eager to speak with the two "fearless sisters" who had played a key role in dismantling the notorious diamond-smuggling ring.

Shirley ducked behind a pillar. "Margaret, they're going to find out we're not real nuns."

Margaret grinned. "Oh, relax. We'll just give them the holy version of events. A few blessings, a lot of charm, and we'll look like saints."

Laframboise sighed. "I'm not covering for you if you lie to the press."

Margaret winked. "Who, me? I'm practically a saint."

As the media storm raged outside, Mother Superior Marie summoned them into her office.

She sat behind her desk, arms crossed, glaring at the two women like they were misbehaving schoolchildren.

"You brought danger to my parish," Marie began, her voice sharp. "You lied, you stole, and you turned this holy place into a crime scene."

Margaret smiled nervously. "But we also... stopped a major crime syndicate?"

Shirley added quickly, "And saved lives! That has to count for something, right?"

Marie sighed, her stern face softening just a fraction. "Against my better judgment, I must admit... you did good. But don't mistake this for forgiveness. You still have penance to serve."

Margaret grinned. "Scrubbing floors?"

"Scrubbing floors," Marie confirmed. "And polishing every pew."

Shirley groaned. "Can't we at least get a medal?"

Later that day, Laframboise returned with unexpected news. "The higher-ups were impressed," he said, standing in the parish courtyard. "You two caused chaos, but you also helped us take down one of the largest diamond theft operations in the country. They want to offer you a deal."

Margaret tilted her head. "A deal?"

"You'll stay out of jail," Laframboise explained, "if you agree to... consult on a few future cases. Think of it as community service. But with law enforcement."

Shirley's eyes widened. "You mean... we'd work with the police?"

Margaret's grin spread like wildfire. "Undercover Nuns—official consultants. I *love* it."

Laframboise sighed. "I can't believe I'm saying this, but... yes."

That night, Margaret and Shirley sat in their tiny parish room, staring at a single diamond they had "accidentally" forgotten to return. It sparkled under the lamplight, a reminder of all the trouble—and fortune—they'd encountered.

"Do we... give it back?" Shirley asked quietly.

Margaret leaned back on the bed, twirling the gem between her fingers. "We could. Or we could keep it. A little nest egg, you know. For emergencies."

Shirley frowned. "We've had enough emergencies to last a lifetime."

Margaret chuckled. "True. Maybe this is our reminder of how far we've come."

With a sigh, she placed the diamond in the hollowed-out Bible. "Fine. It stays hidden. No funny business."

Shirley smirked. "Funny business is all we do."

Two days later, the parish held a "thank you" service for the sisters. The city of Cornwall people, now seeing them as heroes rather than con artists, brought flowers, cards, and homemade pies. Father Maloney even gave them a blessing—though he made sure to remind them to "walk the straight path."

Margaret whispered to Shirley as they accepted a basket of muffins. "See? We're beloved."

"Until they find out you sold 'miracle water' that was just tap water," Shirley muttered.

Margaret winked. "Details."

Before leaving, Laframboise met them on the church steps. "You two are... something else," he said with a faint smile. "If you ever pull another stunt like this, I'll personally arrest you. But for now... thanks."

Margaret grinned. "You're welcome, Detective. And hey—if you ever need a blessing, you know where to find us."

Shirley added, "Preferably *not* in a mob warehouse next time."

As the day came to a close, Margaret and Shirley sat in the empty church, watching the sun cast warm light through the stained glass. For once, there was silence—no mobsters, no detectives, no chaos.

"Do you ever think about what's next?" Shirley asked softly.

Margaret smiled. "Every day. But whatever comes next, we'll face it together. Partners in crime—er, faith."

Undercover Nuns

Shirley chuckled. "I don't know if we're saints or sinners."

Margaret leaned back, closing her eyes. "Maybe a little of both."

Just as they were about to leave, Mother Superior entered with a letter. "This arrived for you," she said, handing it to Margaret.

Margaret tore it open. The letter was brief, typed on expensive stationery:
"We know what you did. We'll be in touch. – V"

Shirley gasped. "The Viper?! He's still out there?"

Margaret's grin widened. "Oh, sister... looks like our work isn't done yet."

Shirley groaned. "I need a vacation."

Margaret chuckled, tucking the letter into her sleeve. "Vacation? We're just getting started."

THE END – For Now

Author Biography:

Merle Pyke is an avid storyteller who has developed a strong passion for fantasy and adventure throughout his life. He has perpetually been captivated by the impact of imagination and the allure of storytelling. He is convinced that tales possess the power to carry readers to different worlds, teach valuable lessons, and inspire creativity. Beyond his writing activities, Merle finds joy in spending quality time with his family and enjoying a delightful cup of coffee.

https://www.amazon.ca/s?k=merle+pyke
https://books.by/pyke-books-publishing

<u>Illustrator Biography:</u>

Hi! I'm Stacey Johnson, a passionate illustrator with a love for digital art, sketching. My journey as an artist began at a young age, and over the years, I have honed my skills to express emotions, stories, and vibrant visuals through my work.

When not drawing, Stacey Johnson enjoys spending time with her husband, children, and of course doodling on every blank piece of paper she can find.

Undercover Nuns

Other books written by Merle Pyke...

- A Fighting Chance
- Brea-Lyn My Friend
- Elmer the Clumsy Ninja Warrior
- Handstands and Heartbeats
- Harlow, Froggy, and the Magical Pond
- Keegan
- The Magic in Room 109
- My Runaway Shadow
- Aleah
- Little Mino has a Wish
- My Runaway Dinosaur
- Dino Disaster
- My Substitute Monster
- Pizza Surprise
- Serenidy and the Blue Winged Fairy
- Serenidy and the Jumping Frog
- The Book of Magical Whispers
- The Japanese Legend of Emperor Moo
- The Fairy Princesses and the Dragon's Secret
- The Magic Yarn
- The Kohen Series:
  - Kohen – King of the Playground
  - Kohen – The Peacemaker
  - Kohen – The Peacekeeper
- Princess Gracelynn and the Enchanted Forest
- Undercover Nuns

More to come...

www.ingramcontent.com/pod-product-compliance
Lightning Source LLC
Chambersburg PA
CBHW060137050426
42448CB00010B/2176